Prais~ ~ ~~ *~~ ~~~~ ~~~~~~~~*

"The remarkable poems in ... y
from the ambitious task h ... e
are poems that are not coi ... 's
of 'the torn, spun world,' where encounters with another can feel like a perfect
absence.' Still, Dechane's poems never wallow in despair. Instead, the poet does
the hard work of discovering in loss the possibility of transformation: 'I have
seen / new colors bloom / in its collapse.' Dechane eschews sentimentality, but
never abandons his belief that meaning can be found 'in this present dimness.'
What makes these poems such worthy companions for the journey ahead is the
generosity of Dechane's vision. 'Imagine a new city / with an old village / in its
heart,' he writes. We want to follow him there."

> —Margaret Mackinnon, author of *The Invented Child* and
> *Afternoon in Cartago*

"In keenly alert and attentive poems, Michael Dechane's full-length debut,
The Long Invisible, reaches into nature and place, capturing all that fills the
senses: 'even the door left / open, how it touches / its latch bolt softly / upon
the strike plate…tap and tap and tap / like a slow heart / still learning to abide.'
These clear-eyed, lyric meditations take the reader from the dissolution of a
relationship, through a time of grounding focused on fond memories, then to a
new relationship and the art of being fully present in the here and now. Poem
after beautiful poem, *The Long Invisible* takes quotidian moments and makes
them visible, wondrous, and worthy of the reader's attention."

> —Aaron Caycedo-Kimura, author of *Common Grace*

"Each time I turn to Michael Dechane's *The Long Invisible*, I have to remind
myself that it's his first book. A debut so wise and searching, so finely crafted
and convincing, is rare indeed. This one, full of elegies and praise songs, recalls
Jack Gilbert as it maps the human heart with aching acuity and James Wright as
it renders the natural world in a revelatory lyric somehow both lush and spare.
Its speaker is full grown in the best sense, with a keen awareness of what's at
stake in the smallest, most ordinary moments and the capacity to attend to
the seismic shifts—the endings and beginnings—that lend a life weight and
meaning. In fearless but delicate pursuit of usable insight into the distances
between self and other and the bridges that sometimes span those gaps, the

collection starts with loss and ends with new love. 'Sometimes,' the poet writes, 'we have to begin again,' and while there is grief here, there is also hope. Dechane offers us, in particular, the hope that saying 'the burning, unsaid thing' can help us keep what's vital, survive our losses, and begin again as many times as we must."

—Melissa Crowe, author of *Lo* and *Dear Terror, Dear Splendor*

"In the poem, 'Spring Dictation,' nature's personified voice declares, 'May beauty confront you,' which is the case throughout Michael Dechane's rewarding debut collection. Made mellifluent by heightened language and seemingly genuine emotion, *The Long Invisible* is personal without being gratuitously confessional, yet engagingly universal via its sometimes dark odyssey of remembrance and sometimes incandescent flights of fancy—the poet's leitmotifs being aptly, continually carried by elegant lines thus: 'Into the barest beginning / of a breeze, one heron luffs.'"

—Claude Wilkinson, author of *Marvelous Light*

"In *The Long Invisible*, Michael Dechane presses language to *fathom* the obscure waters of human relationship, to *sound* the still depths beneath our perplexing voyage that can so often appear to be solitary. To dwell with these poems is to find a companionable voice—a lovely and consoling music—to accompany our own difficult passages. At the heart of these poems is a hunger to apprehend an intimacy that belies our apparent isolations."

—Scott Cairns, author of *Slow Pilgrim: The Collected Poems*

The Long Invisible

Michael Dechane

Wildhouse
Poetry

For Bob Cording

whose encouragement and lovingkindness
helped me believe that I belong

Contents

III

I

Love lasts by not lasting.
— *Jack Gilbert*

No Fortune

Below the wrack the tide
collapsed in ripples,
in the merest waves.
It died in the sound,
a deck of cards
slowly being shuffled.
He looked at the waves.
He tried to hear them.
The night brought more
from its cupboard of darkness.
The blackened water gave
nothing, not a sign, no way
someone so torn should take.
But there he waited anyway
as a little thing about to break.

Everything

I told her everything
but after the impossible heat
where we decide and don't
to betray love, to grind away
vows, how can we recreate
for the ones we have wounded
what we thought, what *really* happened?
We can't, even with the fine details
these photos and furtive notes provide;
our blow-by-blow depictions
told through the fire and sweat
now, of a body flooding with all the shame
and sorrows of our hearts, our minds.
All our evidences are not enough
to satisfy their broken-hearted *why?*
I'm not sure there's anything worse than that.
But when everything wasn't everything,
when I had to say again, *I'm sorry.*
There's more. And I told her.
I couldn't risk, not even then,
to say the last, bitterest bits.
No, those had to go deeper inside
the funhouse rooms of my hidden life
where there are secrets we keep that keep us
alive in the gifts that can only be ours,
and there are the secrets that make us sick.
What kind of truth sets us free?
Why do we need to know, and be known?
How much everything does that cost?

Park Bench Report

A passing car's pyramid of sound.
An August wind troubles a sessile oak.

A dog's bark bites nine holes in the night.
Then the oak tree resumes its summer muttering.

A train strains away on steel under half a moon.
Back up burble the breezy leaves.

A bitter memory of desire drowns everything.
An August wind troubles a sessile oak.

Jake's Parade

The best fire we had in those days was the night
at Jake and Donna's place. It was bitter
cold but we built the bonfire up high, then higher.
Jake was a little drunk when he came laughing
mostly falling down the stairs of the deck
with the Papasan chair from their living room.
Let's burn it, he roared, and we roared back
with the flames when he threw it on and raised
a three-story column of wild, perishing ash
against the darkness still expanding
between the flares of diminishing stars.
I always hated that chair, he announced
as we laughed with relish, in disbelief
as Donna nodded, for once agreed.
Everyone stood up and backed away a bit,
and in the multiplying heat we began to see
what he'd done, what he'd started. It turned out
there were other things in the house Jake hated
so he became his own parade and we the town
that cheered him on. Letters he found and a half-
finished painting. There were books that no longer
worked for him, then the wobbly bookcase tumbled in.
The more he found to burn, the better our fire
seemed to like it and lick its quickening lips.
What I remember most is the goodness of our faces
together, even in that uneven light, once more
before our bonds and vows began to vanish
between us, smoke against a darkened sky. And
the guitar. I hear its last soft sounds the fire played
as each taut string unmoored from its burning bridge.

I Ask All the Brittle Hours

The days we gave each other were bright
poems, pure but unpronounceable then.
Collapsed with you in those fall nights, I imagined
wildflowers springing up through the floor,
rooted on the tabletop, all of the places
we made love giving up heady bouquets
as if we had brought summer inside to stay.
As if we could overthrow autumn
or the descending sadness with its flaring
inevitabilities. There will be a day
I ask all the brittle hours I was given
to say what has remained of the myriad ways
I knew beauty and when I truly lived
in the fullness of love. On that day
the hours will remind me of the city lights
burning holes in the darkness of the hillside
outside our bedroom window. September
shadows from the pine tormented in the wind
as it played, with passion, a silent, midnight *allegro*
over the creamy pool of our bodies in that bed.
How we lay, without speaking, awake at the edge.

The Waters Under the Bridge

He had questions no one wanted
when their therapist started talking
about the need for building a bridge.
Did they know eleven men died
constructing the Golden Gate? And, how much
do you think it costs to maintain a bridge?
So, he helped build the bridge in spite
of his unvoiced misgivings. They stacked up
their hopes, promises, and other flotsam
from the wrack in just an hour, on Tuesdays.
And the most amazing thing was: it held.
She could get from her island to his.
Nobody died. They found they might
afford to keep the thing up after all—
if they could stick to a budget for once.
But before long they began exacting tolls.
Traffic tapered off. He was furious with her.
She felt the facets of his martyr complex
might even outnumber his savior complex,
but mostly she felt sad, trying to believe
their life together could really be this hard.
I will die on my pitiful island, he thought
to himself one day alone, dejected
and in pain from his utter lack
of someone to pull bravely from some fire.
Then a bottle washed up with a message
curled inside. Oh mysterious suffering!
He knew she had sent it, but why, *why*
hadn't she written anything? Why must he
guess what she needed? The blank note
clamped between his teeth, he dove in,
the whole ocean ready to swallow him.

Two Carp in a Bowl

All day they hold their tongues
but when the last guest leaves
and the lights go off in their room
they let fly once more.

I saw you looking at that Kali goddess today,
ogling all those arms and legs, she says.

Quit your fishing and get off my scales,
he fires back. *So what if I looked at her?*
When was the last time you touched me?

Suck grass, you bastard, she seethes.
You always act like it's my fault
I'm affixed to this side of our bowl.
I want to go home, she says, and starts to cry.

He hates it when she does this,
so he yells: *You think I wanted to leave?*
I was happier in the mud under the river!

This isn't all about you! she screams.

And he rolls the one eye he has.
And she glares back with hers.
On and on they go in the frozen
suggestion of circling one another,
the green gulf between them never closing.

When the docent comes again,
turns on the light, they begin another day
under the reflecting glass and gaze
of happy people shuffling past
their case with its little sign:

> *Celadon bowl, 12th century, China,*
> *with double-fish motif in unglazed relief,*
> *a symbol of marital harmony.*

9

Because I Love Twice at Once

No sleep and my night thoughts thicken.
So I come to this window
naked, where winter pours in.
Here is a tang my skin remembers.
I turn and watch my lover, lost to me
for a while on her own pillowy island.
But still, I can't see the problem.
Somewhere, far into the night,
another love sleeps. Or stands
at her own window. I can never know,
and even now it is not a thought of her
face that surfaces but rain that I feel
arriving somewhere between us
in an empty, cut field, moving at first
like a sheer curtain darkened
and shaken by a slight breeze coming in
after the last sunlight falls out of it.
But then the rain becomes a matador's cape,
ruffled and draped
over the great sweeping arm
of the torn, spun world.
And once more, my body remembers
how ardor is the thing with horns.

Black Bear

I told you about the bear
how it came padding through
the tall grass along the fence line
sundown last night. Its dark bulk
like a perfect absence, animate.
I tried to describe what it felt like
to be unseen. Still. Caught between
impulses to keep safe, to see more.
When you called me, I told you
how much these nights you're gone
hurt me in ways it's hard to say.
And you said you didn't know
when you might be coming back.
We let a silence bloom between us.
I'm writing to say what I could not.
How I trailed it, downhill, trembling
to the treeline tracing the creek bed.
How the bear paused to scent the air
as I was caught, exposed on open ground.
It swayed in a sprawl of yellow crocuses
growing dim in the blossoming night,
like a greater darkness, claiming candles.
Everything melted in a moment, beyond sight.
I was afraid. It was there, then it wasn't.

The Mailman

He keeps bringing her the bills
and offers for new credit cards
and fliers about Grand Reopenings.
He's forgotten the last time she got a letter,
a personal word from someone she knows.
Foolish as it seems, he brings her things
addressed to the Current Resident because
it feels worse for him to arrive with nothing.
Every few weeks at a dinner they arrange,
or before they fold into their cars after therapy,
in the narrowing spaces when they are
face to face and he might manage to say what
he wants so much to tell her, what he keeps
quietly, stupidly saying instead is
Here's the mail that came for you.
And she takes it with a smile and thanks him
like he really is the mailman—a face she knows
belongs to someone she does not know—
and she puts it in her purse.

On the Causeway Seawall

Last spring, drag screaming, I caught a big snook
here on the causeway seawall and let it go.

Next July, with beers on our spare comforter,
legs dangling over the rocks and water

we'll sit close under the sky torn open,
our cheers for the fireworks finale

absorbed without return into that night.
Tonight? I don't know why I came back here.

There's a whole world I can go on seeing
without you, but sometimes I need to feel

along the chipped edge of what's explainable,
come back to this brim of where we ended.

Tampa is a spangled hyphen,
two inches of the horizon.

A weak, quarter moon over the bay pulls
one way, the gone sun, its own direction.

The water, taut in the tension and light,
becomes a meadow of obsidian.

In this neap tide memory, what surfaces
is the appalling quiet wound in the sea.

It stretches, undulates, and then contracts.
It presses against, then off, the seawall

languidly. I can almost hear silence.
But in slow recurrence, the water siphons

out again, through the riprap's dark pockets.
That sound, systolic. Tonight, mnemonic.

A Happenstance

If a poem is a dark and unfamiliar room
we enter fumbling for a light switch,
then I am thankful for this bench
just inside the door closing, clicking, locked
from the outside, in the abandoned hallway.
Perhaps we can sit together for a while.
Maybe our eyes will help us to perceive
what could be in this present dimness.
Whatever is before us, I once arranged.
So what? In here, I'm the same as you.
I need to make what I can of what there is.
Do you have children? Remember
how everything we create may transform
into what we can't even pretend to control.
I'm sorry to say it like that just now,
since it seems metaphor got us into this mess
but is so unlikely to get us out.
Also, I never want to argue with you
again. I'm starting to remember now.
Those tottering, darker shadows are poems
and piles of rotten bits I wrote once
you left. I tried to forget about this
room and all its dust and debris after
I shoveled their stinky strophes inside to expire.
What are the odds, both of us wandering in here?
This is serious, though—*stop laughing*.
No windows. No way out. No unlikely rescue.
And it's a bit late to conjure up a skylight
and some skinny, shaking ladder for escape,
wouldn't you say? I would say so.
Yes. That is precisely what I would say.
A trap door? If there is one, I bet it is well-hidden
and opens by a secret, diabolical mechanism.
One of us could slip out as the other dozes so
it's easy to imagine how this could become a place
where nobody talks about leaving anymore.

On the Sunshine Skyway Bridge

Bright, clear mornings from the bridge's crest,
the hidden contours of Tampa Bay
emerge. Sandbars surface in the low tides.
Mangroves crowning oyster beds make islands.
The white, sandy bottom reflects the light
where it tumbles into the deep cut
of the shipping channel. I'm terrified
of heights but this is my morning commute
as one of the 60,000 who grind each day:
up this grade, then whistling down.
In the average month, someone stops to heave
themself from the peak of the long span's deck.
They come from all over. This is our high ground.
One of every seven will wake up
after the jump which often breaks every bone.
So, some morning I could be one of those
passing by as they arrive at the edge
of whatever has held them up so far.
I want to hope and I want to believe
that some courage I cannot see from here
will rise up and I will stop.
I cannot imagine that moment—
only that I may want to be there with them,
suspended in the light with so far left to fall.

Why Am I Kinder to Your Memory

Why am I kinder to your memory
than I was to you? Or so generous
to your future self? What opens in me
now to want their good with such tenderness?

Under my heart there must be a cellar
holding all I could not feel in your arms.
In dark bottles, filled by some vintner,
lies the love from vines on a hidden farm

which could be growing anything this time
of year—mealy pears or another house
we could not live in. But I would not mind
a bit more loss: let's toast what's been. Aroused,

my heart pours out but cannot quite decant
this amity, so late, of no account.

Expedition Notes

I cannot say what I expect to find
canoeing up the spring-fed river
we once floated down together. It's hard
paddling against the current carrying
the memory of how we drifted
and slipped quick and quiet through
the runs and riffles in love that summer.

Already I question this daydream quest.
I am sunburned, cursing, horsefly food
and only just arrived at the sandy
bend where we camped with a little fire.

Inside our tent alone, I watch a storm
sear the night sky outside in bright lashes
that press the raving silhouettes
of trees in flashes on the leaking walls.

The things I brought are sodden and ruined
this morning. I have decided to leave
everything and press on upstream.

Deepening evening now. I've come all the way
back to where this part of our story began.

I cannot say what I expect to find
each time I arrive here at the spring
where we put in together. Faint stars riddle
the cypress canopy and ropes of moss.

I think of Sisyphus and Shackleton,
those better and hardier men who knew
recurrence and the truth of a compass.

Palmetto fronds keep up their susurrus
here at the brink, the bank, the dark welling
water pulses, surfaces in a rush,
a cold and helpless throb that is forever
running off through the young arms of the night.

Paper Wasp

That summer our windows were wide open
hands begging any breeze of the pitiless
heat each sludgy day of June. I remember

a wasp headbutting the globe of the light
hung in our living room the afternoon
we left for vacation.

The night we got home,
I found it drying at the foot of our bed,
its bruised head drooped, its long legs scrolled inward,

wrapped in the finest hairs and stuck with dust,
dead, its magnificent, brickle body
still intact, if not preserved. As we were

eating our way along Portugal's coast
sampling prawns and seafood cataplana,
the pastel de nata, not really talking,

it slowly concussed itself against the glass
of the invisible panes that kept it
locked in the stillness we left looking for.

Less may portend than I once believed.
But these days, I can see the ways we needed
some death, an opened window, and a breeze.

Last Look, Amsterdam

Roar.
Airborn.
A final ascent.

The shuffling white cloud
of hungry ibis lifting
and falling behind
the creased face of a farmer
resolute on his tractor.
He is making new lines
in the mud of the old lines.

A lattice of water creasing
the diminishing green
as polders reflect
weak light strained
by close, gray clouds.
Lead ditches etched,
ready to gleam.

Cloud.
Clear sky.
A radiant coverlet.

Aubade

Do not go, little hour.
Salt pinched from the sea
of Time—do not go.

My kiss prayed all night
against your gray arrival,
but now my Jacob mouth
clings to you, breaking light.

This silence before
love pulls itself
apart, against
the current of its own
longing, is the most terrible
silence I know.

My mouth is a lake
with a hole in its bed.
All my words run back,
drain down into my heart
where no one can hear them.

I want you with me
in this wordless place,
but lie still
in your dream.
Do not bring us closer
to the unlocked door.

From the hidden waters
of the fallen lake
I will draw up the words.

Little hour before the ache—
never go. Be always here,
a rest she may lie in
some other lonely day.

The Long Invisible

Last night it rained
and more hangs over us
this morning. It's good
the way these open
windows welcome
a cooling breeze
between seasons
and how it seems
to play with the steam
of my coffee cup.
I think of rollicking dogs
in the long invisible
seedy wet grass
of a topography beginning
only now, to surface, to be.
It's easy to imagine
things like this before
the peace of the day breaks.
It's good to let this be
my only news for now:
rain and more rain,
a freshening inside
my soughing house.
All of this is very good,
even the door left
open, how it touches
its latch bolt softly
upon the strike plate
when each breezy episode
rushes in, and then subsides:
tap and tap and tap
like a slow heart
still learning to abide.

II

Starting here, what do you want to remember?
— *William Stafford*

New Year's Day

Broken streams of anhingas
winging low over the lake
like the words of poems
I could not make last year.
Gulls carve the new air,
the light of another first
morning. Into the barest beginning
of a breeze, one heron luffs.

If nothing else will happen
to witness so much alive
may be enough. Even now
one anhinga lands. Its black curves
swallow their reflections on the surface
where many others rise and dive.

Birthright

Sometimes a nameless
sadness I do not understand
arrives in the afternoon
after all the good color
has fallen out of the sky.
Maybe that will happen today.
I watch purling veins of smoke
rise from my neighbor's chimney.
I think of my father and his wish
for us to scatter his remains
on a distant river we loved to fish
where it goes fresh to brackish.
Heat shimmer blurs the morning
and the essential lines of trees
along the banks of this river.
Their January hands are empty
of everything but crows,
those silhouette descendants
of the ones that cried
above the window and crib
in my father's first memory.
When he cried, no one came.
Heat rises, dissipates. Shadows
wing downstream. Under the ice
that thickens and blurs its face,
the river, pure and undeterred
is still insisting on its way.

Pier 60

Hurricane Billion Dollar Betsy roaring
toward New Orleans will kill 73 people
tomorrow, but this afternoon, September 8th,
1965, all these Florida boys see
are bigger waves in the Gulf than they've ever seen.
Denny, Rob, Sammy, and my dad are four wet cores
of themselves—fifteen, growing into thicker skins—
but today, they're freer than they know as they run
down the pier, wet feet slapping concrete, grinning
into the rain-shot gusts, through the turnstile outside
the locked-up bait shop, easing their eely bodies through
with homemade plywood skimming boards they've painted
with cartoon devils, sailors, and heroes. Their dads,
at home smoking and whiskey-shot, don't give a shit
where they've gone or what they do if they don't get caught.
So, as they've done all morning, they race to the end
of the pier and look out over the last railing.
Big, angry swells, all the way to the horizon.
It's a two-story drop onto the charging crests
and closer to three in the troughs. By now they know
what happens if you catch one low—you bottom out,
your board's nose catches in the sand, you flip, you roll,
get chewed up, shell-raked, laid open, pumped full of salt,
and crash land on the hard-packed sand. Your buddies laugh.
You do it again. They're all a little bloody.
They cup and pass around a last damp cigarette
from their stash on the beach. Behind them, the long dark
limbs of the Australian pines in the parking lot
wave almost frantically in this wind, as if they know
what's coming. Vietnam. A gunshot suicide.
A drunk driver on a Christmas morning. A long string
of blue and purple clouds roil over the ocean.
Their cherry flares. Smoke rips in streams from their faces,
and they're laughing, ready to vault in.

Red Kapok Tree

Bloom petals
like tongues
torn out mouths
full of exuberance
full of suffering.
Your red reminds
me year by year
of all that was
or never said.

April Thieving

Another week. Maybe two.
Then, all the nests we found
last fall will wink away
behind fresh green eyeshadow.

But the moon may remind me.
Just now, it seems to burn
and rest in a confusion
of budded cottonwood limbs.

A reflected occlusion rising
over our obscuring roofs.
Like a home above, it swells
with all we find to lose.

Purple Heart

(Tradescantia pallida)

Haze of a boy's sleep
as he wakes up within
a cool humidity and breeze
disturbing thin muslin curtains
his grandmother sewed
to soften her guest room.
Beyond their opaque flutter
the green glass jalousie
windowpanes lend color
to the morning light. Beyond
them, the assembled shades
under a live oak's fullness.
And beyond everything
below the boy's window,
his grandmother hums and tends
her Purple Heart and azaleas.
It rises and greets him,
this nameless lingering
song where her feet are still
draped in an amethyst wave.

Cemetery Soundscape

April layers of birdsong
I both understand and don't:
Looking for sex? Build me a nest!

Unasked bells say their expected piece
at the hour from a shingled steeple,
a needle in the peering sky.

Hydraulic drone of a backhoe
as it scoops another hingeless door
to another flower-sprouting cellar.

A good working silence
between two men that stand beside,
helping out the hole.

When their shovel blades shear
in the earth made raw again
that sound pairs contrapuntal

to another man who is tamping down
a different mound, contracting the grave
to what looks like leveled ground.

The cloud-muted roar of a departing
jet settles, welcome among these other rows
of the waiting in this absorbing place.

Quiet rises, even as everything continues.
I am listening where it might seem
no one speaks, except the birds, insisting.

Between Oceans

— for Jason

Arcing, electric blue tentacles
of fireworks tonight find a memory
finning around in my dark and deep.

Our sixteenth summer. Daytona Beach.
Blush of our salt-sun-razed bodies.
Full dark. Cold wind. Warm sand.

The distant lamps of the pier, strung to nothing
and a gash of light carved the sky.
Another. Us silent. Then more. Meteors

tracing synapses of the night mind.
Had we ever been so confronted
by the violent unexpected waiting in our lives?

The Perseids hypnotized us out of time.
Maybe we thought things like this keep
happening, and there would be nothing to forget.

We lay there forever, between oceans,
the galactic above, the Atlantic at our feet,
only decades, deaths, and a blue flare from here.

August

Forever the bell month
ringing us back
into primped classrooms.
Summer's coda.
Sweating usher
of a shoulder season.
What an unfair face
you gave us, August,
canceling our freedom
so slowly, still
shimmering heat.
31 sputtering
gas-jet days,
my early lessons
in the pains of lingering.
Even now, you are
the calendar's kiln
firing the majestic
images I carry.
Citrine cherry
tomatoes crowning
our shaggy garden.
Faces of poets
tending a bonfire
on Whidbey Island.
Ice beds
and splayed mackerel
in the Algarve markets.
Dust, resplendent,
rising at sunset
after an Oklahoma tractor.

Instructions to My Future Self

If the time has come to remember your life
will only be one thoughtless breath gulped in
and this seeping fight against the exhalation,
be as kind as you can. Go back to the water.
Set out in your kayak, and paddle down the sun.
If it's going to, let the moon rise on you.
Over the deep channels drift, eyes raised
to count only the unnecessary stars, long dead,
the light blasted out their collapsed and burning
mouths and stretched these millions of years,
fallen at last into your eyes, through a universe
in your mind. How much have they truly died?
Be depleted. Done, alone, exposed, keep under
the mercy of the night. Pray once but well enough
for a wind to come with a rhythm lapping
capless waves on the hull that holds you.
Let down your little folding anchor and feel
the wind-dried rope that warms your hands,
the salted air now steady, steady on your face.
Let your anchor mark its furrow in the mud.
Keep as you can the sound the wind makes.
Cast in the waves each word you could not speak.

Something So Obvious

In the hardest days
with their outstretched nights,
whatever is beautiful
in the world recedes.
Light leaches from everything
we see, then. We can't touch
ordinary goodnesses we might have
let buoy us. All of it fails. Sometimes,
we have to begin again
with something so obvious
and tired as the sunrise.
The wind in long grass.
The light holding back
our eyes from what is under
the surface of the water.
Then, the same light giving
a wrinkled glimpse of stones,
silt, and dark fronds waving
when we shift our stance
half a pace, or even turn
the angle of our face.
Some belief that goodness keeps,
that it might come back one day—
what could that mean today
when there is only the sun
returning in a flat peach wash,
the burning usher of another
Tuesday, coming in with the clanks
and grinding sounds of the city
shaking itself off, reanimating?
A waking we might observe
in colors we may discern
as all the life we lost burns out
of sight, beyond us now, as memory.

Jacaranda

The white sinew under bark,
wet through with water suckled
from its dark round of earth, is torn,
not in weakness, but in tender
resolution to give way, be broken
by the weight of blossom,
by the fluttering violet it was given,
a clutch of amethysts to bear
before the sun for us this little while.

The Gathered, Made Ready

A yellow tomato comes apart at the seam
my knife makes. This skin: how can it hold
so well so much? I salt the weeping flesh
that reflects this morning light.

Rye bread, just turned, just lightly become
my toast—I break it, too, and it blesses
the tomato with fine crumbs. I smell seeds
of a plant I have never seen.

The egg, softly boiled, my reverent joy
for peeling it—I hold it warm and whole
outside its shattered shell. It was another thing
before, will open again, be another, yet.

Lapsang Souchong

In China someone closed your leaves
in tiny fists that grip the smoke
that dried you. A world away I wait
by another fire. The cup waits
with me. The little blue dragon
that lives in my stove does his work.
The kettle begins to sing
the one note of its one song.
The day becomes itself beyond
the glass of the kitchen window.
I pour the kettle and you become
again yourself, but haunted now
by memory of a distant fire.
In this steam rising as smoke
I remember myself, who I was,
before I knew all night the flames,
before I tasted you or knew your name.

September

Hurricane dregs come rousing the morning
roughly combing these gasping green mountains.

Gusts pry the loosened edges of the trees,
find little ways inside our reckless summer life.

This tattered blue skeleton's rattling
breath will hush all the emerald candle flames.

On Blue Mountains

The wind from the west is still
unmaking these mountains:
each branch and blade tip points
toward the sea, the sun that rises.
From the summit I see around myself.
See winter fallen along the spine
of crowning ridge, red spray bouquets
of rowanberries, bleeding mountain ash.
Below, other trees raise the full stain of fall.
And still the green of summer's coalescence
in the valley floor, the edge of my sight.
I have been standing here for years
seeing where I was, and had been,
with a splitting ache to name
that place where all I've seen began,
myself unknowing seed of that day
in me, held so long in bud.

Recurrence

The gentle current of Jenkin's Creek
carried me by the muddy bank
I crouched on as a boy, dip-netting
blue crabs lured by a chicken thigh.
Past the last bridge before the Gulf.
Into the sawgrass and saltmarsh smell.
Edging along the wildness of palms
shaggy and bent in unkempt sloughs.
Thankfully, the fish weren't biting.
I laid my fly rod down.
I laid my paddle down.
I lay my body down.
I let the smooth current take and turn me
as I remembered the sky
with eyes embarrassed for staying away
so long. Once more, clouds textured
the blue beyond above. Below me, the clear
fresh water retraced the final turns.
I closed my eyes and fell asleep.
A small, insistent movement came.
The merest waves made a new sound.
And I woke up somewhere between,
in the confluence of creek and sea,
one of the thin places our bodies find,
and rocked in the tension, perfectly held.

All Those Other Nights

Moon wedge blaring without restraint.
Salt-thick air blows balmy, then
cool, troubling the dry palm trees
overhead. They flick the darker black
of their fronds against the outer deep.
The persistence of the ocean
calling its own name along the shore.
This is all it takes for me to feel
my life folded upon itself, tonight
touching all those other nights
that held the briefness of my being
there as easily as disintegrating stars.
Nights with so many versions of myself
I did and did not walk away from,
like the starfish that breaks itself
in half and then regrows its own past.
Michaels and Michaels, a chorus of us
in the relentless moon's diminishment.

After Your Trip

Now, it could be wherever you have
gone has changed, if not who you are
then how you are. Maybe that's why
the rooms of your house feel more
like someone else's as you step inside.
But probably not. It's so unlikely
whatever you did while you were busy
not gazing at the ocean gazing back
at you burning on your beach
vacation has rearranged something
in your deep places. What will you do now
you've set your bruised bags down
in the unstirred air of the living room?
That name doesn't feel right,
does it? You might think,
This isn't where I live. I don't come alive
here before the television, night after night.
There is more time than we know.
There is less time for this, though,
than we guess. A few more breaths.
Then all the shimmer of strangeness blanketing
your things, the life you left, and are once more
about to pick up, will lift and dissipate.
Why? You cannot say. You only know
those reasons in the unlocked rooms
waiting beyond what you can yet imagine
now inside yourself. A final, unmarked breath
and all this will become mostly normal
again. You'll see. It's happened many times.
You've gone. Somehow, returned. You go on.

Gladiolus

— for Ava

The slow wither
of this bled out
gladiolus
in our big vase
on the table
doesn't make dying
beautiful. But
I have to say
for five mornings
now I have seen
new colors bloom
in its collapse.
Incarnadine
streaks of ruined
flowers hang like
threads, suggesting
sutures on the white
wall behind them.
The drying tips
all along its
inflorescence
have become brown
as baby flesh
and delicate.
The green leaves give.
The water turns.
Multiplying
opacities.
I sip coffee
and remember
a perfect word
my young niece made
once in delight—
it's *glorgeous*.

Upbringing

How I come up
we might say
where I am from
which now I love
for insisting on a present
tense inside what we remember
about the dimming past,
almost as if it still is
happening, our "early training."
Come is becoming
before my eyes
a disobedience we love,
having grown up enough
to put off our first grammars.
None of this is what I want
to say about what it meant
to be so small
when we learned
what we learned.
Jesus is furious.
He's raging
at the door
of his dear friend
newly dead. He bellows
Come out!
And rotting Lazarus does.
And I am supposed to
believe something
about grief-love-power
in this resurrection
lesson from my childhood.
Out of the depths
it rises up once more,
that dirty, beautiful
verb that won't go back

to sleep. No, *come*
commands and cajoles.
It remembers
where we are
from is where we are,
still carrying everything
we were given
and not given—
all we can't
cast off so easily
as burial clothes.
A word that knows.
How we all come up.
A syllable in our deep.
How we all come out.
I believe in this
late, kind upbringing of all.

III

… give it, give it all, give it now.

— *Annie Dillard*

City Tour

Imagine a new city
with an old village
in its heart. You begin
walking where the fields give
way to the latest fringe
of homes. Do not build
a map. Remember the way
it feels to follow only desire.
Let your body take
all that you want forward,
if only in your mind. Press
farther into this blazing
morning of your new city.

Notice the rising rows
and rows of beige apartments,
how the face of each seems
the same as you
pass through the long grid
of your unfurling streets.
See people weeding gardens.
Reading in windows. Waiting
for buses. Count the blocks.
Keep walking. Take all day.
Take months. Take until
middle age, getting to know
the fountains and benches,
the neighborhoods in this
clarifying outpost of your mind.

Arrive, one day, at the edge
of the old village. *Who laid
the brick of these streets,
and how long ago?* perhaps you
wonder when you realize

the sharpness of every corner
here has been lost. Follow
the river as it curls one
bank like the back of a cat
along the inner curve
of the road. Move through
the shade and light pocketed
below an ancient row of oaks.

Greet the shopkeepers you know
by now this morning after years
of wandering in the old village
of your new city, always exploring
and stopping at sidewalk cafes.
Consider people. Small surprise,
some of the passersby remind you
of lovers, their faces here are sharp,
unweathered corners of memory
after all. You don't live here any more
than Ithaca. There is no home for you
to return to, nights in this city
you have lived inside your entire life.

Keep walking and it will be
like this morning one day
in the first urgencies of spring
ambling under new canopies
of the ancient oaks. You may see
an alleyway you never noticed
before. *Who knows?* Sometimes
the mysterious bricklayers make new
things in the night as you wander.
The alley is thick with shadows.
Dewy west windows mutely frame its mouth.
Of course you will go into its coolness.

Feel, inside that narrowing space,
a gentle stillness preserved
with an invitation somehow beyond
articulation to hold being held.
The alley curves out of your sight
then eases back, bending another way
almost in playfulness, and coming to this:
wisteria, hung in the full sun.
It pours the fullness of itself,
scenting an advancing breeze
that floods, in a moment, your city
and the entirety of its valley.

Sojourn

I could watch this snow and abide for the rest
of the pared night falling into the bucket
of light the streetlamp brought out precisely
for this reason. It reminds me of the way
I love to see a salty crew of workers
build or unbuild things, with the unfeigned ease
which comes at last ten thousand times after
the uncertain step, those first clumsy strokes.
Attending the snow's arrival relieves me
of building my own work inside tonight.
How kindly the world lays aside my tools
and restores to me some open hands.
The scene in this window becomes a window
for seeing again the beloved face
of a lake I am forever still beside.
Over its dark depths a breeze in the morning
would lift tiny peaks for the light to play on.
The dazzle in the elemental is
inexhaustible and waiting for me,
both capturing and refracting my gaze
beside the lake, before this snow, somewhere
I am too drowsy to imagine, now
quieted by the sight of what descends
unasked to make anyway a blanket.

Birthday Pastoral

The wide tongue of meadow tapers
to a bight in Riceville Road
near the volunteer fire department.

Driving through that quick, sweeping curve
you have the best view of the valley
for a second—for another—for one more.

I cannot choose what I love
most, the surfeit spirit of summer
rioting over this ground, or the fence.

Long wands of Queen Anne's lace
hold forth among the insistent
stalks of sky-drop chicory blooms.

The fence has two parts: its rotting posts
and the breathing emptinesses between them
where the rusted barbed wire was stripped away.

And across the road, behind a proper gate,
matte-black cows rove like wonderful things
that happened to me, but I have since forgotten.

This little turn in the road is a good place
to stop for the long, wild, full-throated view
early and quiet, another last morning.

Starling

— *in memory of John Wyllie*

I haven't thought of starlings
in months, maybe longer.
But looking up just now
from a letter I'm writing to another
friend who is learning how to die—
a letter I do not know
how to finish—starlings.
They fill my winter-bleached grass
like rustling, light-flecked galaxies.
How many thoughts has it taken
to displace their last visitation
from my brimming mind?
They make me remember: to be
present means forgetting
some while, at least, so much.
One bird bolts lightly into
the shadow of a cypress
and then bursts through,
back into this pale light
unblenched and iridescent.

Ladyfish

Imagine a greyhound
without its cumbersome legs.
Just bone and speed
a vibrating tendon
a flashing diminution.
It's the final refinement,
what's left
when everything
that wasn't fish
is whittled.

It shatters the saltwater
ceiling of its world,
tailwalks and flails against
the insistence of the line
and my eight-weight fly rod,
against the biting deception
of a white Clouser minnow
Marty tied and mailed to me.

It drives itself,
a writhing silver spike,
into the morning
alive between memories
of outrageous sex
and Stendahl's syndrome
in Kunsthaus Zürich.

A sprung coil
a furious arch
something said at last—
each time it erupts
above the oblivious
waves, it says more
about the wild violence
of what is beautiful
and coursing everywhere
under the skins
of the world.

Seventh-Grade Story

We must unlearn the constellations to see the stars.
But going back toward childhood will not help.
  — Jack Gilbert

Every kid on that blistering, humid bus could smell
the ripe, fresh dog shit someone must have stepped in.
Even with all the windows down that afternoon,
even more pungent than our collective, tween stank,
it hit us. God, Jesus almighty—*please not me*—
I thought as I surreptitiously checked my high-top soles.
Shit. I stared hard out of my own window
in feigned, far-off contemplation. Like a kettle
of vultures, the kids around me circled closer, sniffing,
until Chris—that freckled, doughy fuck—my best friend
by default because he was the only one
who ever talked without some taunt to seventh-grade,
trailer-trash me—that poor kid sold me out.
A chorus of laughter, and as quickly as they'd closed in,
my peers, all my fellow Pineview Panthers, repelled,
pinching the noses of their exaggerated faces in disgust.
Except for Ken. He came at me, a pair of biceps,
a mullet, and a sneer, an unwitting eighth-grade cliche.
He pinned me in my seat, his face in mine,
the ashtray of his mouth opened in exertion
as he pried the offending shoe from my foot
and launched it out a window, into the ditch
and everyone else cheered. The bus driver
barreled on, down Highway 54. It was over then
for them. Once more, I stared hard out of my own window
without any filter for shame, managing somehow
not to cry and offer them another reason
to give me any attention. How could I have known,
even then, fabricating the simplest lie I could think of
for when my father would ask about the mystery
of my missing shoe—*I lost it*—how could I
know that staring hard out of your own window

is absolutely essential if you ever want to become
or keep being a poet? Even now, I must do it
to tell you this. Of course I couldn't know then
any more than I knew how necessary it is
to wreck the sentimental. When it crumples, finally,
the real story, the hiding life, is free to emerge.
I stumbled down the steps and through
the folding door. The tears came, then. At the end
of my street I saw a bright bird of paradise swaying
in the shade of its own place in a neighbor's flowerbed.
The click of grasshoppers in the dryness of the field
sounded as the bus engine died off completely.
In that new silence, I walked home slowly in the dust
of our graded, limestone, dead-end road.
One soft step in my sock, then a hard one in my shoe,
as I became a perfect, burning iamb.

Driving Into the Morning

She could have been asleep
half hidden in the grass
at the shoulder of the road.
The young doe's body wracked,
doubled in a dancer's folding grace
and cold beyond the curve
come sharp at the river bight
just after the Edgar farm.
Her ocher face seems unmarred.
A dark eye open toward me
idling in the road. The fresh cavity
of her belly, already eaten,
gapes mercifully away.
It's easier to imagine her
moonless, losing purchase
and tumbled down
the white face of this rotting
limestone bluff instead of crushed
clean-cracked in half, her spine broken
without scratching the brush guard
on some jacked-up dually,
flags screaming along its bed,
wounding the softness of the night.

Round After Round

Nobody asks bartenders for advice anymore.
The woman in seat 3? She won't ask me
about her love problems. Once she got
what she ordered, she cranked up
the old show *Nonchalant* for the benefit
of the guy two seats over in 5. Bored
with her life, she's fingering everything slow:
the rim of her wine glass, now the stem,
the edge of her napkin. She is blotting
her weathered lips, gazing everywhere,
settled on nothing, face open as a vault.
I won't bother starting a tab for her.
I see how all this goes—how he buys
that Syrah for her when he moves
to the incidental empty seat at 4.
It won't take much more scotch and soda
for the eyes to roll, the talk to turn to romance—
or what this pair of guzzling clichés pass for it.
And me? I pour fuel for shaky platitudes.
An hour to closing these two will be three glasses
past telling one another how done with love
they are, done reciting tired scripts
of what they have learned, all the mistakes
they won't ever make again as they sit,
lean closer in to their next drink.
I don't hate them, but it's as if I'm a co-producer
in the longest running show of human history.
I'm tired of watching us be so bad to one another,
making sure I hear nothing, keeping
my mouth shut to save a tip, save this job.
Let me ask you something, if you don't mind.
How much do you think it matters that I want
to give each of them something
they will never ask for: an embrace that gives
something back for what was taken,
round after round of poured-out love,
something to help us all see the world again,
say really what is love for our first time?

59

Supplications

Give me a splash of light.
A pine splinter in the heel.
My name in a mouth I love.
The wren, crumpled in the flowerbed.

Give me the unexpected
dash of suffering or delight
to shiver me awake, again.
Dim the ordinary enough.

Let the rising shadows breathe.
These spare moments to be
and to be here with you
are everything I have.

Give me the mountain on fire
in the plummet of our day,
its fierce, jagged print
upon the blackening blue.

Ode to the Mullet

Dumb sea bullets.
   One mindless swerve
a panic of fish
   pushed like steel
shavings away
   from a magnet
before an osprey's
   shadow. Grey meat
so oily your
   sole redemption
was a heavy rub
   and being hung
in a smoker.
   Until the day
with my fly rod
   waist-deep wading
I saw you sown
   in swells of cresting
waves backlit with
   the rising sun
transmuting you
   leaden tokens
into pure coin
   flung up from a
sunken kingdom.

Lovestruck Montage

The poet, inside, is in love
with the airy parade of birds
appearing in the spirit and colors
of little flags set free of their countries.
They cling to the feeder, turning slowly
in the bare limbs of a Kousa dogwood.
Standing at the kitchen window
beside a banneton of proving dough,
an electric kettle beginning to steam,
and wooden spoons, settled in their jar,
the poet eats a grilled rye sandwich
and pries open, one by one,
pistachios.
He attends the incoming
red-bellied woodpecker.
Soon, a hazelnut in its beak
like a jewel in the tension
of soldered pendant prongs.
Ice encasing the branch tips' drips.
Four chickadees arrive and vie
for the best purchase
and a choice seed. The sun,
mid-afternoon careening in late
January descent, gilds from behind
the edges of a golden-crowned kinglet.
Happily and simply it seems,
the bobbing charcoal jots of juncos
sift the snow below the feeder
for what has fallen to them.
Oh, the whole world cannot glisten
in this melting scene but places
of the dogwood's mottled bark
do against all that yawns beyond it
just the way, within, the poet does.

Three Times She Peels a Grapefruit

The dimpled peel comes off in patches.
There is no sound like this sound, being torn.
My lover's hands can pull apart a sun.

She turns the pith down like a sheet.
How quietly it surrenders covering.
She feels no hurry for this undressing.

A red moon peers through its ruined envelope.
We hear a chrysalis-shucking whisper.
I trace this arc of longing as she holds the edge.

Only one lithe wall remains between us
and the taste. She leaves barely enough
to hold what may never be held again.

With unselfconscious grace
she makes these shambles and plunders
the bitter fraction. She keeps giving

all of her eyes' attention to her book beside me
in our bed. I watch her hand find my mouth
to offer the glad collapse of a hundred fullnesses.

Yield

You know the way new lovers touch
for no reason. Giving themselves
over completely to an obliterating
hymn of desire. The body becomes, again,

a foreign land they have always wanted
to explore. With their hands, two idiots
behind ten aching lamps, they foray.

A forearm. The nape. Lovely corrugations
of ribs and the hidden, ordinary
wonders holding us together. We remember
after all, there is reason enough.

Those ruddy, grinning, clay-stained farmers
are planting touch by touch everything
they will have to fill a first winter's table.

Noontime Tableau

Unless some fatal thing visits me
in my living room where I plan
to read and work all afternoon
this bowl of soup won't be my last meal
in this life. Is there any reason
not to savor its spoonfuls
or how it smells as if it were?
Yes, why not praise the noodles,
how they surface like ripened kelp
in this tiny, brothy ocean?
Or the ways they resist being
lifted by my inadequate spoon.
Radiant carrot—my mouth doesn't deserve
you, at ease on your beansprout couch.
Sweet wheel. Tenderroot.
If you were a woman, I would ask
to make love to you on our kitchen island
here on the well-scored butcher block
where I whittled your peel.
Oh, soup. You rapturous gathering
of the world's nibbling bits,
elixir against the dull afternoon sun.
I meet the stare of a halved egg,
softly boiled, with my tongue
in the warm yellow gum of its iris.
Mushrooms? What can I say about you?
I admire your greedy ways
drawing in oils and spice while giving
me your earthy perfume. Even this
riot of ginger cannot drown your aroma.
Nor can the humbled, undone garlic,
its binding split, its thin pages
boiled to a poem's translucence.
And unseen in the depths—the duck.
The breast, seared last night, is resting,
sliced today with its last offering of blood.

What I've Come to Love

The texture of finely grated ginger.

Fernet's herbal alchemy,
its tincture when I close the day.

All the surprising variegations in a cloud.

And seven black cows my neighbor keeps.

Some modest disappointments—
the kind that help me
know I've asked too much
and not enough.

Those parts of myself I kept
locked up on a kind of death row.

A list that needs
to interrupt me into attentiveness.

How this, a poem,
can move me beyond
what I knew, then further,
past what I can imagine.

I've come to love portals
into universes that do not exist
until we say they do.

Whoever you are, I love
your power. I hope it gives life
and sustains goodness for you, and everyone
connected to you: every one of us.

I know what I've come to love
may not love me back
yet. May I keep on loving
then. Keep practicing on stones,
long grass in the grips of a wind,
water, every way that it might be.

What a help that will be to me
as I turn, at last, to you.
The one I could not know
I was meant and made to love.
I am a stranger, a faceless other,
but you have invited me in.
You give me this time with you.
Forgive me for not believing sooner
in the gift of generosity,
the hospitable spirit you have
harbored within, all these years, for us.

Ode to the Pelican

With your brain the size of a sea grape,
you glide ten feet wide just inches above
the wild, rolling skin of the sea. Or tip to tail, hunting
in threes and fives, you make motorcycle gangs
on sky highways. Even when you clown
on the fishing pier, walking clumsily
down the railing to beg my grunts and pinfish,   ·
little snappers or some greenback bait,
my admiration leaps senseless as a mullet
when you fix the wedding band of your eye on me.
And I love your motionless moves, your napping
on one leg, the collapsed dump truck of your mouth
laid over your shoulder in repose as casually
as the way you float your buoyant bones
on crest and trough for as long as you need to rest.
But mostly I can't keep from praising
your signature dives—those banks and upturns,
the calculated stalls before you plunge and pierce
and surface with some wriggling thing
you have found in me. In your profile, I see the form
that wrought your name: *pelekys*,
the double-bitted axe of Zeus. And when you fall
and go under, I could believe you were thrown
by the invisible hand of some god with whom
you share the sky. But even more so
when you beat the water with your wings and rise.

Another of Love's Arrangements

First, the blind baton leaps
up, arching, arcs to touch
its worn place on the roof.
It presses harder there
the more we feel to say.
Soft smash of flesh allows
what had been kept below
into the yawning pit
of the warming orchestra.

In the second movement
many euphoniums
remind us with a note
of their surprising lives
in the back of our throats.
That gutswell sound lays down
the flabbergasted tongue.
In the heart of our word
sounds a groan that has known
each taut mile of desire.

The coda comes quickly
in a heave suggesting
the sweet, loitering buzz
of a kiss we needed.
That little vibrato echoes
what we have been given,
what we give, when
the lip leans in to press
its hidden tenderness
upon the windblown teeth.

Coming to Terms

I am thinking of a word we do not know
yet. Our bodies have begun to form
shapes for the sounds of this coining entry
in the unwritable dictionary of new lovers.
It is not a secret, or even private, but
unmistakably and only ours, this
becoming expression of us we find
by the groaning of our hands and hips.
A term our mouths mold together
with a blazing, unpronounceable vowel.
We articulate the edges of virgin plosives
hidden in the breath between us,
in a florid pair of blue gutturals sounding
your deep need with mine to say it again,
to say it again in the fleeting tongue
of fingers and skin.

Resound

I can hear the woman I love
more than steak and frites and apple fritters,
more than a winter mountainside coming green,
more than anything I might ever make,
more than any of you and all of you together.
She is chopping carrots and peeling beets.
She is undoing the garlic on the dark stone
countertops of our kitchen. Soon the vegetables
will brown, then crisp, then burn, completely inedible.
We don't know this yet. But now, there is still time.
She is tending here in the deepening evening
the work to make us dinner. It's been a shitty day
and there is a beautiful door closed between us.
Clear pine. Simple lines. Softly oiled, matte.
I closed it to lie down for a nap. I want to feel
a few unhurried breaths. Remember
how much so much of this doesn't matter.
Remember how much what does, does.
Instead of sleep, the good, soft sounds of her hands
reach me, dimmed some by these years and the door.
The day with all that's wrong, is. And yet, I rest here
in the sound of the one I love more than anyone
alive, staining pink her sure and perfect hands.

Meditation on the Heart

And then, one day, you see
the copper teakettle on the stove
settled on its iron throne, precisely
in its place in the kitchen landscape.
Where, all these years, it has been
let's not say faithfully. Not exactly.
But in its home, hallowed within
a scene so familiar it seems known.
The faint blue streaks of verdigris,
even the dullness of the handle,
become beautiful in this long-arriving
moment of recognition. Beneath
its dinge in the pockets of its dents glows
an undiminished gleam. Every morning
it has been lifted, filled, and carried.
Each day, it pours. But you so rarely
touch it between its burning hours. Now
it is you that is filled as you long
for what you cannot see or say but sing.

Night Swim

— for Regan

The full, white-fired eye of the moon
meets mine over the sawtooth crest
of an evergreen horizon. The night sky is
a field thick with the emergent burning
speeches of the stars. A riot of wildflowers
enflamed in the roaring negation of space.
I taste woodsmoke. The river inside me
rises as your face and voice return
and take a choice place at the table
set for us in the great hall of my mind.
How hungry the dark, the wan moon, seem
for our feast and all we have come to know
of love. I hear the longing of the world
stir in a sweep of wind that bends
the limbs of trees, still so full of summer,
to rub the way I hear the cricket.
Some nearby oak or elm creaks upon itself
and I remember us, outside the boathouse,
stripped, and the water-rocked song
of the dock we slipped from into the black
lake water lit with a lavender-tinted moon.
The warm slicks of our bodies found each other.
Our mouths met—a bright galaxy was born.
Legs kicking against the deep, we held hands
and one another, fearless, into the morning.

Deep Unto Deep

You are the wild untethered
color of the blossom
petals stampeding the garden
gate and the way they pave
beauty along this weary road
exposed in soft escape
by the first lights of morning.
I believe the jasmine vine
is longing bloom by bloom
in the night for another.
The name that thickens breath.
Your syllables fill the dark
cup of my mouth. Undone,
the peach-pink sound of you
burgeons unruly along my tongue.

New Epistemologies

We gave long, generous time
to unlearning the inadequate
ways of knowing. I mean words
doing their best distillation
of what the conscious mind decided.

Therapy was helping. We clapped,
cried, and cheered the good, endless,
clanging parade of the heart's wisdom:
desires in every shade, disappointments,
each way to love, and every shame.
But the eyes of our hearts grew weary.

And even before we began
subatomic tigers, perfect
in miniature, glossy black stripes
were breeding, dividing in our skin,
thriving in the unseen savannah
waiting in that tall, gold grass
to have the body's say.

Spring Dictation

The dogwood blooms became
creamy, opened envelopes

yesterday, gladly unburdened
of their urgent letters for us.

Be every color alive, they said.

Do not exhaust yourselves
in the grip of little things.

Be candent roving flames
who savor the darkening world.

May beauty confront you.

Be the two hearts of one
fire blossoming at twilight.

In These Last Minutes

Say the burning unsaid thing.
Say what there is time left for.
Quarter no cleverness
in these last minutes.

Say the names of the unloved.
Say slowly those names you hate.
Empty the great gulch,
the scorched earth of your heart.

Say then the old adversary knocks.
Say every fierceness you rehearsed
balks before his ugly, benevolent face.
What now? Do you need to know why

forgiveness heals before pronouncing some—
say the burning unsaid thing.

Acknowledgments

I'm humbled and remain amazed to see the list of first homes for many of these poems. To every reader and editor of these journals, thank you!

"Aubade," "Jacaranda," and "Lapsang Souchong" (*Image*)
"Cemetery Soundscape" (*Spiritus*)
"Gladiolus" (*Ruminate*)
"Instructions to My Future Self" (*Cumberland River Review*)
"Jake's Parade" (*Atlanta Review*)
"Ladyfish" (*Lake Effect*)
"No Fortune" (*Pilgrimage Press*)
"On Blue Mountains" and "The Gathered, Made Ready" (*St. Katherine Review*)
"Ode to the Mullet," "On the Causeway Seawall" (*Hampden-Sydney Review*)
"Paper Wasp," "Why Am I Kinder to Your Memory" (*The Mustard Review*)
"Pier 60" (*The Maine Review*)
"Purple Heart" (*The Forum*)
"Seventh Grade Story" (*The American Poetry Review*)
"Sojourn" (*Ekstasis*)
"The Long Invisible" (*Tar River Poetry*)
"The Mailman" (*Southern Poetry Review*)
"Three Times She Peels a Grapefruit" (*Valparaiso Poetry Review*)
"Two Carp in a Bowl" (*The Ekphrastic Review*)
"Upbringing" (*Relief*)

I'm especially grateful to Kirsten Miles, who runs the 30/30 Project for Tupelo Press. The chance to participate in that project birthed early drafts of poems included in this collection: "All Those Other Nights," "August," "Between Oceans," "Birthday Pastoral," "Black Bear," "Upbringing," and "What I've Come to Love". Kirsten's hospitality in Port Angeles, WA, through the Gentle House residency, was such a gift during the editing of this manuscript.

My publisher, Wesley Wildman, and the editorial Board at Wildhouse Publishing, believe in this work enough to bring it to you, readers, and I won't get past my gratitude for that.

My editor, Mark Burrows, was a delight and keen help from our first correspondence. He brought a finer edge to the manuscript and many of these poems—and has proven to be such cheerful company in the details and confusions of publishing my debut collection. Thank you, Mark!

Melody Stanford Martin's beautiful cover design makes me feel seen and heard as a poet. That her work incorporates the glorgeous artwork of my friend John Sarra—a deliriously fine painter, woodworker, teacher, poet, skateboarder, and human being—thrills me to my core. Thank you, John, for your friendship and work that does what poetry cannot.

My dearest cousin, Stephanie Beaty, happens to be the best portraiture photographer I know. No one else could take a better frame of me. For a lifetime of spirited play and then mucking around in palmettos, cypress swamp, and mangroves to catch my headshot in that wilder Florida we both love—thank you, cuz!

Since poetry and trying to make poems has threaded my life as least as long as I can remember, I thought I knew what a poem was. What poems do in the world. What animates their stuffing and turns them into, if not things alive, at least things that help us live. Then I read "A Troubled and Troubling Mirror: On Poetry" an essay by Scott Cairns in *A Syllable of Water*. The insistences it hardly contains incinerated 30 years of my mostly thoughtless thinking about poems. And, in the same breath, it offered me such a compelling vision for what a poem—and maybe even a poet—could be. The poems gathered here only bear the early marks learned late that poems are less shrines and more like springs. More like the seep on the hill above our house that feeds, in every season, the roar and course of the French Broad River, far below. For the mighty helpful corrective, then, and good humor to season the work, and a sober induction into the life of letters, and your lectures on Dillard, and your book on suffering, and your introduction to faith that reveres mystery, and your poems that be what you preach, and an overdue appreciation for Lyle Lovett, I thank you from the depths, Scott.

I knew within hours of meeting my peers in the Seattle Pacific University MFA program—soon to be transplanted to Whitworth University—that I had found my people. Charlotte Donlon, Sarah Orner, Amy Peterson, Rachel Sheild, Hallie Waugh, Luke and Megan Gilstrap, Catherine Ricketts, Annelise Jolley, Jane Scharl, Celinda Olive, Andrea Rooks, Arthur Boers, Janay Garrick, Sarah Sanderson, Julie Sumner, Dawn Morrow, Jeffery and Anne Overstreet, Tripp Lybrand, River Jordan, and others carried me through the rigors of graduate school, an exceptional season of soul-searching, and, miraculously, soul-finding. There's no better company for the journey than all of you. Keep the Whidbey fires burning, beloveds.

Erin Griffin-Collum, Rachael Schmid, and Andrew Graney reshaped my experience of friendship during our MFA studies, and then through the pandemic, as I was living abroad. Long, long video calls every Friday for years. So many of the poems in this collection are better because of them. I'm especially indebted to brilliant, huge-hearted Erin, one of the most gifted editors I know, who considered an early draft of this book with such curiosity and care. I love you all.

Bruce Ray Smith quietly attended to me as a trusted friend and brother through divorces, shuffling around the globe, writing doldrums, my first pangs of spiritual displacement, and a decade of scribbling. For your steadfast care, and our inexhaustible love of reading, fishing, cooking, Florida stories, laughter, and faithfulness—thank you, Bruce.

David Lindrum has been wrestling over what writing is with me since the fall of '96. No one asks a better question or gives a better invitation to the best things in life than David. I owe you more than I could hope to begin to list, my friend.

My Zürich writing group buddies—Dustin, Julya, Ali, Jim, Nikki, Matt, Joanna, Marit, Lyndsay, and Ella—were the best company as I was working out new poems in a strange and wonderful place. Their reading and friendship were such a help to me and this work.

It hurts me to compress here all that some of the great teachers of my life gave me—but this book and my path with poetry wouldn't exist without each of them.

Courtenay O'Connell, my elementary school Library Media Specialist, stirred and stretched our ideas about metaphor making—and recorded our early efforts. What a gift, in my 40's, to meet, by way of YouTube, third-grade Michael trying to work out what to compare myself to in the unspooling universe.

Julia Drummond, my eighth-grade English teacher, worked hard to little effect to help me diagram sentences. But she praised my writing and encouraged me to enter a Modern Woodmen of America essay contest. Her encouragement to the shaky and prone-to-shame new kid at school was salvific.

In high school, Betty Williams suffered my scandalous personal essays with patience and gentle redirection—and gave me better writers to read. Bill Evans gave me a spot on his speech team and my early lessons in reading poems aloud, with an alertness to their terrains of sound and rhythm. I began to know by my body and voice how poems hold their power and what it can mean to offer them to others.

Bill also introduced me to Berry College where I met Dr. Randy Richardson and my real education in poetry began. Shakespeare, Bukowski, Stephen Dunn—Randy handed me who he intuited I needed next. He let his own love for language and what happens when you sit with a poem long enough to internalize its images and ideas help me experience what happens when you read a poem that has read you.

Jeanne Murray Walker amplified all my earlier lessons and helped me fumble my way inside formal poetry. She turned me loose in the wide territories of poems in translation, gave the best advice about publishing work, and has been such an inspiring and generous correspondent well beyond my time at SPU.

And finally, Bob Cording, to whom this collection is dedicated, encouraged me to keep writing poetry 'to have a better life.' He did me the favor of not explaining this so that I might live my way into the joys of giving the world my better attention; of learning to accept people as they actually are; of finding my way toward the truths and depths of our shared humanity. More than anyone else I know, Bob lives these things in astonishing ways. Bob gave me and the work of this collection his patient care, suggestions where it was failing, and the inside-out living and spirit he risks with everyone. I am profoundly thankful to Bob and Colleen Cording for their friendship and enduring kindness to me.

The unswerving love and support—forever—from my brother David and my parents Robin and Art Dechane—has buoyed me through every upheaval, collapse, and celebration in my life. They've each given a lot to help me find my way. Mom gets a double portion of thanks here for ushering me into the holy byways and worlds we meet in the pages of our books. Dad taught me how to be on the water, in the woods, and eventually, with myself. I could never have made a single poem without you both. Thank you, family, for your great, abiding love.

"Three Times She Peels a Grapefruit" is Hillary's poem. That some friendship, love, and respect could survive my failures in our ramshackle years together is one of the greatest wonders of my life. Thank you.

"Aubade" is Caitlin's poem. You gave me—with so much else—the largeness of the world. And my way into a bolder, gentler version of my life. For all of it, and every ounce of adventure—thank you.

Regan gave me a song that would not die. All the new love poems are hers but every poem I've written in the last 20 years owes her something. Love, when our friendship and savory letters bloomed in The Way Back Years, I knew there was something deep and shared and kindred between us. Before I knew the word, I knew you were my *claymate*. You were the only friend I talked about poetry with, and we read the 'pohems' one another wrote, and together we loved the mud it takes between your toes to be sufficiently in the world—enough to find something to say about it. When I published my first poem, you were the first person I told. And so much later, outside of Time, in the heady smells and sunlight of an ancient olive grove—you came once more to mind. I sang out the song you gave me—a keepsake I carried across Our Silent Years and other lives—and you sang back, hours later, from half a world away. Whatever will happen—from here, until—owes most of its joy to you.

Michael Dechane is a poet who carves wooden spoons and indulges his passion for historic home renovation. A "word-tender and wonder-vendor," his work has appeared in *Image*, *Southern Poetry Review*, *Tar River*, *Lake Effect*, *Spiritus*, and elsewhere. In 2020, he was awarded Ruminate's Broadside Poetry Prize. He serves as the VP of Communications on the Board of the North Carolina Poetry Society. With his partner, Regan, he is a custodian of a home built in 1900 in a cove forest on the French Broad River, north of Asheville, NC. Learn more at michaeldechane.com.

This book is set in Optima typeface, developed by the German type-designer and calligrapher Hermann Zapf. Its inspiration came during Zapf's first trip to Italy in 1950. While in Florence he visited the cemetery of the Basilica di Santa Croce and was immediately taken by the design of the lettering found on the old tombstones there. He quickly sketched an early draft of the design on a 1000 lira banknote, and after returning to Frankfurt devoted himself to its development. It was first released as Optima by the D. Stempel AG foundry in 1958 and shortly thereafter by Mergenthaler in the United States. Inspired by classical Roman inscriptions and distinguished by its flared terminals, this typeface is prized for its curves and straights which vary minutely in thickness, providing a graceful and clear impression to the eye.

www.ingramcontent.com/pod-product-compliance
Lightning Source LLC
Chambersburg PA
CBHW031553060525
26234CB00087B/1313